DISCOVER Ancient Rome

by Barbara Brannon

Table of Contents

Introduction	2
Chapter 1 What Was Ancient Rome Like?	4
Chapter 2 How Did the People Live in Ancient Rome?	10
Chapter 3 Why Was Ancient Rome Important?	14
Conclusion	18
Concept Map	20
Glossary	22
Index	24

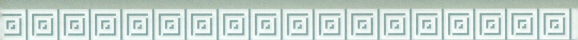

Introduction

Ancient Rome was important. Ancient Rome had an important **civilization**.

▲ Ancient Rome had a civilization.

Words to Know

ancient

civilization

empire

laws

roads

Rome

See the Glossary on page 22.

Chapter 1

What Was Ancient Rome Like?

Ancient Rome had buildings.

▲ Rome had many buildings.

Ancient Rome had emperors.

▲ Rome had emperors.

Ancient Rome had soldiers. Ancient Rome had wars.

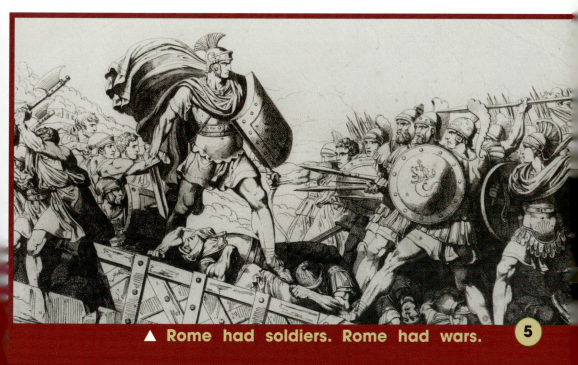

▲ Rome had soldiers. Rome had wars.

Chapter 1

Ancient Rome had art.

▲ Rome had art.

What Was Ancient Rome Like?

Ancient Rome had temples.

IT'S A FACT
Most temples had columns.

▲ Rome had temples.

Chapter 1

Ancient Rome had books. Ancient Rome had maps.

▲ Rome had books.

What Was Ancient Rome Like?

Ancient Rome had gladiators.

▲ **Rome had gladiators.**

Chapter 2

How Did the People Live in Ancient Rome?

Rich people had large houses. Rich people had servants.

▲ Rich people lived in large houses.

Poor people had apartments.

▲ **Poor people lived in apartments.**

All people had plays. All people had contests.

▲ Gladiators fought in the Colosseum.

How Did the People Live in Ancient Rome?

Did You Know?
Romans had contests in the Colosseum. Part of the Colosseum is still in Rome.

▲ The Colosseum was a theater.

Chapter 3

Why Was Ancient Rome Important?

The ancient Romans had gods. The ancient Romans had goddesses.

This is a goddess. ▶

The ancient Romans had **roads**.

▲ This is the Appian Way. This is a road.

The ancient Romans had bridges.

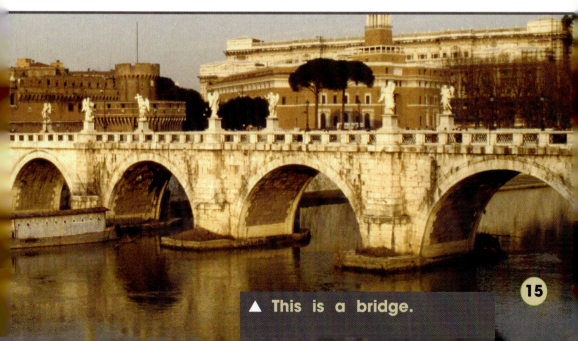

▲ This is a bridge.

Chapter 3

The ancient Romans had **laws**.

▲ This is a court.

Why Was Ancient Rome Important?

The ancient Romans had an **empire**.

▲ This is the empire.

KEY Roman Empire

Conclusion

Ancient Rome had a great civilization.

Concept Map

Ancient Rome

What Was Ancient Rome Like?
- buildings
- emperors
- soldiers
- wars
- art
- temples
- books
- maps
- gladiators

How Did the People Live in Ancient Rome?
- rich people — large houses, servants
- poor people — apartments
- all people — plays, contests

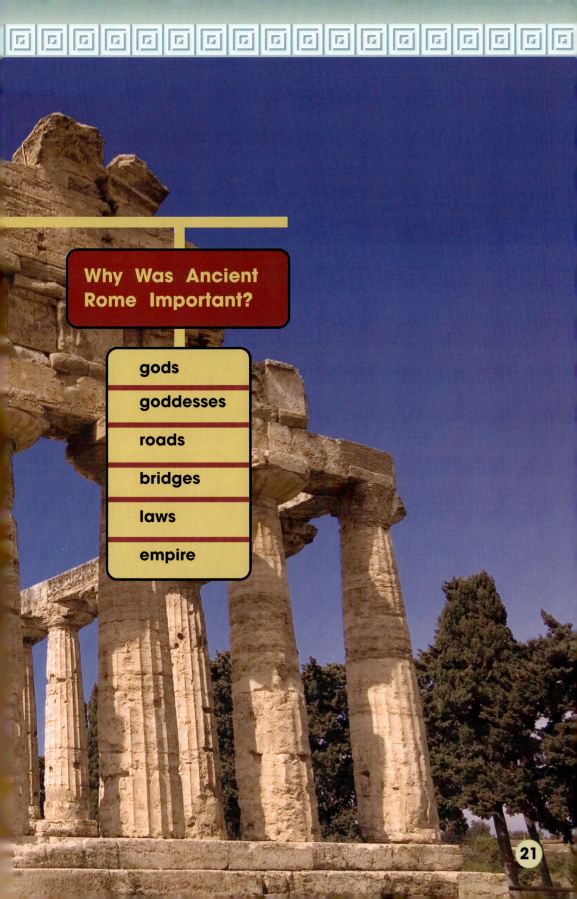

Why Was Ancient Rome Important?

- gods
- goddesses
- roads
- bridges
- laws
- empire

Glossary

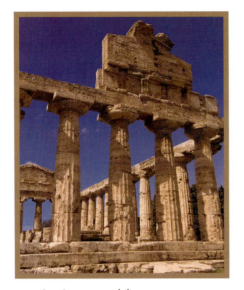

ancient very old

Ancient Rome was important.

civilization a group of people that share ideas about living together

Ancient Rome had a great civilization.

empire lands ruled by an emperor

The ancient Romans had an empire.

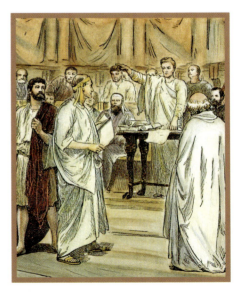

laws rules that govern people

Ancient Rome had laws.

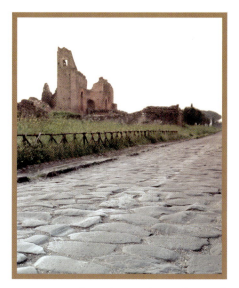

roads paths cleared and used for transportation

*The ancient Romans had **roads**.*

Rome an ancient civilization

*Ancient **Rome** had an important civilization.*

Index

ancient, 2, 4–9, 14–18, 20–21

apartments, 11

art, 6

books, 8

bridges, 15

civilization, 18

contests, 11, 13, 20

emperors, 5, 20

empire, 4, 17, 21

gladiators, 9, 12, 20

gods, 14, 21

houses, 10, 20

laws, 16, 21

plays, 12, 20

roads, 15, 21

Rome, 2, 4–10, 13, 21

servants, 10, 20

soldiers, 5, 20